JACK PRELUTSKY

It's Snowing! It's Snowing!

pictures by **JEANNE TITHERINGTON**

Greenwillow Books, New York

Library of Congress Cataloging in Publication Data
Prelutsky, Jack.   It's snowing! It's snowing!
Summary: A collection of more than a dozen poems
that capture the excitement of winter.
1. Winter — Juvenile poetry.   2. Snow — Juvenile poetry.
3. Children's poetry, American.· [1. Winter — Poetry.
2. Snow — Poetry.   3. American poetry]
I. Titherington, Jeanne, ill.   II. Title.
PS3566.R36I83 1984   811'.54   83-16583
ISBN 0-688-01512-3
ISBN 9-688-01513-1 (lib. bdg.)

In memory of
Marie Weiss,
my grandmother
—J.P.

To Dr. Edmund W. Hardy
et laus Deo
—J.T.

Contents

IT'S SNOWING!
IT'S SNOWING!

It's snowing! It's snowing!
Snow carpets the ground,
the air is a silvery blur
that's whiter than paper,
and whiter than milk,
and whiter than polar bear fur.

It's snowing! It's snowing!
It drifts into mounds,
our car's hidden under a hill,
snow covers the rooftops,
embraces the trees,
and blankets my own windowsill.

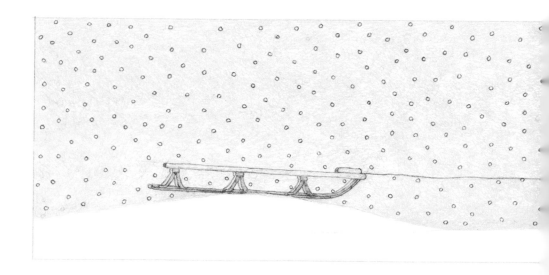

It's snowing! It's snowing!
I run like a hound,
I romp and I roll like a fool.
It's snowing! It's snowing!
And if my luck holds,
this morning they'll close down
the school.

ONE LAST LITTLE LEAF

There's a leaf clinging fast to
    a branch,
though withered, it somehow
    holds on,
and a single bird singing its song,
though all of its kindred have gone.

And as long as that little leaf stays,
and as long as that stubborn
    bird sings,
then autumn remains in the world,
and winter must wait in the wings.

DECEMBER DAYS
ARE SHORT

December days are short, and so
there's not much time to play,
the fun has hardly started
when the sun has gone away.

Today, right after breakfast,
while the sky was growing light,
I ran to meet my friends outside
and have a snowball fight.

We began to build a fortress
then raced our wooden sleds,
we belly-whopped and spun like tops
and tumbled on our heads.

We stopped for lunch, then
    once again
threw snowballs for a while,
we made a giant snowman
with a really silly smile.

We fed some hungry pigeons
and went sliding on the ice,
my mother brought some
    cake for us,
a dog ate half my slice.

We made another snowman
and we finished off our fort,
then suddenly, the sun went down...
December days are short.

SHADOW THOUGHT

The winter sun stays close to me,
it watches where I go,
and my shadow is the shadow
of a giant on the snow.

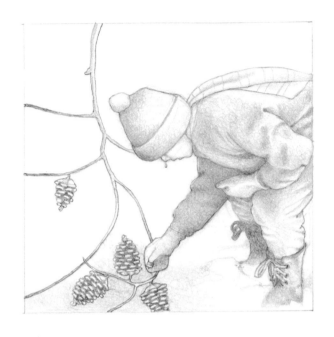

WINTER SIGNS

Winter signs are everywhere,
the winter winds are nipping,
winter snow is in my hair,
my winter nose is dripping.

WINTER'S COME

Winter's come, the trees are bare,
no leaf now whispers to the air,
they've dropped away, and in
    their place
are filmy sheets of icy lace.

No songbird sings, they've long
    since fled,
no feathered wings beat overhead,
no cricket's click or buzz of bees
now serenades the silent trees.

The air is sharp and clean and cold,
the grass has turned from green
    to gold,
in cozy holes beneath the ground
small creatures sleep and make
    no sound.

Upon the frozen earth I lie
and listen to the silent sky,
winter's come, the trees are bare,
no leaf now whispers to the air.

MY MOTHER
TOOK ME SKATING

My mother took me skating
and we glided on the ice,
I wasn't very good at it
and stumbled more than twice.

My mother made a figure eight,
and since it seemed like fun,
I tried a little trick myself
and made a figure one.

MY SNOWMAN HAS
A NOBLE HEAD

My snowman has a noble head,
he's broader than he's tall,
his ears are tin, his eyes are coal,
he has no neck at all.
Beneath his ragged hat he wears
a wig of tangled wool,
his barrel chest is buttoned up,
his belly's rather full.

My snowman has a handsome face
complete with carrot nose,
his arms are long, his legs are short,
he hasn't any toes.

He wields a broom, he puffs a pipe,
his smile is wide and bright,
"He looks like me!" my father says,
you know...he may be right!

I AM FREEZING!

I am freezing! I am freezing!
I am absolutely cold,
I am shivering and shaking
like a pudding in a mold.
There are glaciers in my stomach,
there is sleet inside my bones,
I am colder than the contents
of a million ice-cream cones.

I am freezing! I am freezing!
From my bottom to my top,
all my teeth are clacking madly
and I cannot make them stop.
Oh I cannot feel my fingers,
and I cannot feel my toes,
now my cheeks are frozen solid,
and I think I've lost my nose.

I am freezing! I am freezing!

Inside out and outside in,

every bit of me is chilly,

every single inch of skin,

I have icicles inside me

and my lips are turning blue,

and I'm sneezing as I'm freezing,

for I've caught a cold…

AHCHOOOOOOOOOO!

MY SISTER WOULD NEVER THROW

My sister would never throw
   snowballs at butterflies,
lately, they've not been around,
and certainly not at a dragon
   or unicorn,
both are infrequently found.

SNOWBALLS AT BUTTERFLIES

She cannot throw any at fishes
    or porpoises,
we are quite far from the sea,
and never, no, never at tigers
    or elephants,
she only throws them at me.

MY MOTHER'S GOT ME
BUNDLED UP

My mother's got me bundled up
in tons of winter clothes,
you could not recognize me
if I did not have a nose.
I'd wear much less, but she'd get mad
if I dared disobey her,
so I stay wrapped from head to toe
in layer after layer.

I am wearing extra sweaters,

I am wearing extra socks,

my galoshes are so heavy

that my ankles seem like rocks.

I am wearing scarves and earmuffs,

I am wearing itchy pants,

my legs feel like they're swarming

with a million tiny ants.

My mittens are enormous
and my coat weighs more than me,
my woolen hat and ski mask
make it difficult to see.
It's hard to move, and when I try
I waddle, then I flop,
I'm the living, breathing model
of a walking clothing shop.

STUCK IN THE SNOW

Stuck in the snow,
dad's pickup truck.

"Sorry, dad,
    that's your bad luck."

"Shovel it out!"
he smiled and said.

I guess it's *my*
bad luck instead.

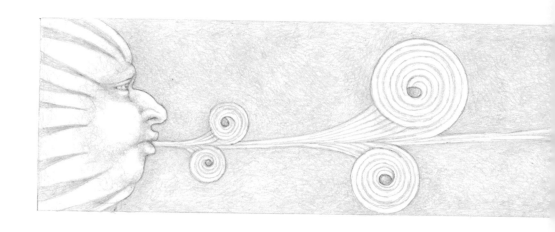

I DO NOT MIND YOU, WINTER WIND

I do not mind you, Winter Wind
when you come whirling by,
to tickle me with snowflakes
drifting softly from the sky.

I do not even mind you
when you nibble at my skin,
scrambling over all of me
attempting to get in.

But when you bowl me over
and I land on my behind,
then I must tell you, Winter Wind,
I mind...I really mind!

40

A SNOWFLAKE FELL

A snowflake fell into my hand,
a tiny, fragile gem,
a frosty crystal flowerlet
with petals, but no stem.

I wondered at the beauty
of its intricate design,
I breathed, the snowflake vanished,
but for moments, it was mine.

WHEN SNOWFLAKES
ARE FLUTTERING

When snowflakes are
fluttering   fluttering   fluttering
down in the cold winter night,

I watch with surprise,

as they fill up my eyes

with uncountable pinpoints of light.

And when they are
BILLOWING BILLOWING BILLOWING
over the ground in the day,

to cover the street with a glistering sheet,

I delight in their lovely display.

When snowflakes are

shimmering shimmering shimmering

gently on top of my hair,

to give me a crown of soft

powdery down,

I wish they would always be there.

But when I am

SHOVELING SHOVELING SHOVELING

till every bit of me aches,

I truly wish then, that I'd never again

see those little white fluttering flakes

THE SNOWMAN'S LAMENT

My snowman sadly bowed
    his head
in March, one sunny day,
and this is what he softly said
before he went away:

"IN THE MIDDLE OF DECEMBER
I WAS HANDSOME, ROUND,
      AND TALL,
NOW I HARDLY CAN REMEMBER
THOSE DECEMBER DAYS AT ALL.
OH MY STOMACH'S STARTED
      SHRINKING,
I AM LOSING ALL MY FORM,
AND I'M THINKING AS I'M
      SHRINKING
THAT I WISH IT WEREN'T WARM.

"I CAN FEEL MY SHOULDERS
    STOOPING
AS MY BODY'S GETTING THIN,
MY NOSE HAS STARTED
    DROOPING
AND MY MOUTH HAS LOST
    ITS GRIN,
I AM SURELY GETTING
    SHORTER,
THERE IS LITTLE LEFT
    OF ME,
MY HEAD IS BUT A QUARTER
OF THE SIZE IT USED TO BE.

"I AM GETTING HARD OF HEARING
AND MY VISION'S LITTLE USE,
FOR MY EARS ARE DISAPPEARING
AND MY EYES ARE COMING LOOSE.
THROUGH THE ICY WEEKS
    OF WINTER
I STOOD PROUDER THAN A KING,
NOW I'M THINNER THAN
    A SPLINTER,
WINTER'S MELTING INTO SPRING!"

JACK PRELUTSKY was born and raised in New York City, but now makes his home in Albuquerque, New Mexico. He has been entertaining young readers for years with his funny and original books of poetry, including *Zoo Doings, The Baby Uggs Are Hatching, The Sheriff of Rottenshot, Rolling Harvey Down the Hill,* and three ALA Notable books: *The Queen of Eene, The Snopp on the Sidewalk,* and *Nightmares: Poems to Trouble Your Sleep.* His Greenwillow Read-alone Books include *It's Christmas, It's Halloween, It's Thanksgiving, Rainy Rainy Saturday, It's Valentine's Day,* and *What I Did Last Summer.*

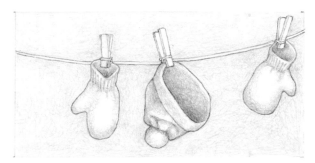

JEANNE TITHERINGTON was born in New York City in 1951 and now lives in Portland, Maine. She is a graduate of both the Portland School of Art and the University of Maine. She has illustrated several books for older children.